Stomachaches

Dr. Alvin Silverstein,

Virginia Silverstein, and

Laura Silverstein Nunn

My Health

Franklin Watts

A Division of Scholastic Inc.

New York • Toronto • London • Auckland • Sydney

Mexico City • New Delhi • Hong Kong

Danbury, Connecticut

Photographs © 2002: Custom Medical Stock Photo: 20, 29; Nance S. Trueworthy: 24; PhotoEdit: 30 (Bill Aron), 38 (Mary Kate Denny), 32 (Rachel Epstein), 18, 31 (Myrleen Ferguson Cate), 8 (Tony Freeman), 4 (Spencer Grant), 14 (Jeff Greenberg), 19 (Michael Newman), 6 (Merritt Vincent), 16 (David Young-Wolff); The Image Works/Bob Daemmrich: 25; Visuals Unlimited: 21 (Nancy P. Alexander), 10 (John D. Cunningham), 40 (Mark E. Gibson), 28 (Given Imaging), 22, 36 (Jeff Greenberg), 23 (Fred E. Hossler), 34 (Gregg Ozzo), 27 (SIU), 26.

Cartoons by Rick Stromoski

Library of Congress Cataloging-in-Publication Data

Silverstein, Alvin.
    Stomachaches / by Dr. Alvin Silverstein, Virginia Silverstein, and Laura Silverstein Nunn.
        p. (cm).—(My Health)
    Includes bibliographical references and index.
    Contents: My stomach hurts! — How digestion works — Is it something you ate? — Going to the doctor — Treating stomachaches — Take care of yourself.
    ISBN 0-531-12192-5 (lib. bdg.)   0-531-16238-9 (pbk.)
    1. Stomach—Diseases—Juvenile literature. [1. Digestion. 2. Stomach—Diseases.] I. Title: Stomachaches. II. Silverstein, Virginia B. III. Nunn, Laura Silverstein. IV. Title. V. Series.
RC817.S54 2003
616.3′3—dc21   2002001730

Contents

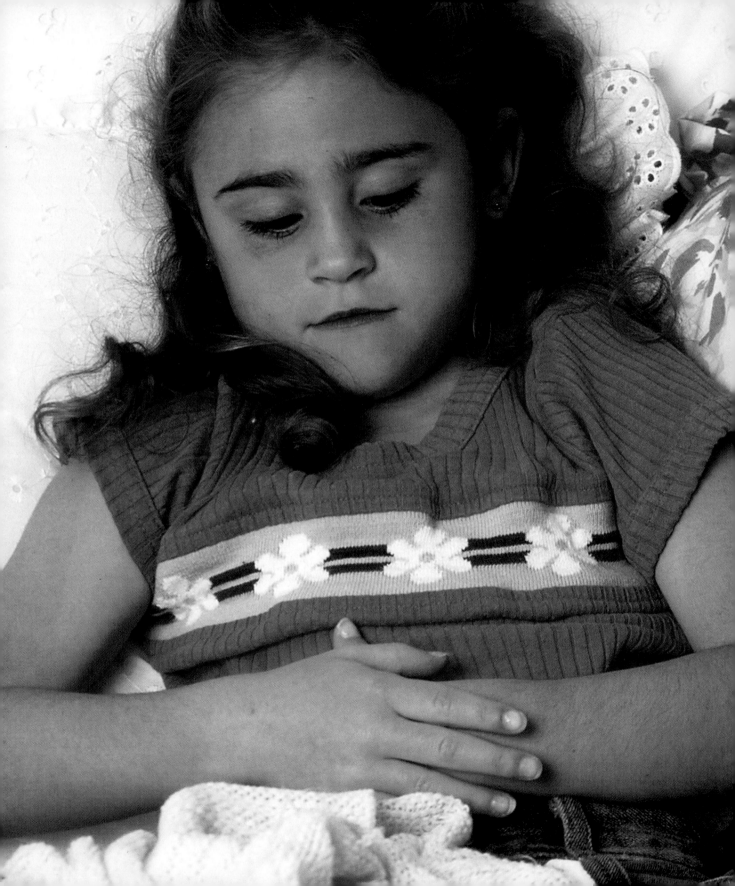

My Stomach Hurts!

How would you like a big, juicy cheeseburger loaded with onions, a plate of french fries, and a tall milk shake? That sounds like a delicious meal. But for some people, this great-tasting meal could lead to something bad—a stomachache.

If you have ever had a stomachache, you're not alone. Most people have had an upset stomach at some time in their lives. Some stomachaches can make you feel uncomfortable; others are so painful that you bend over and clutch your stomach.

An ache or pain is a sign that something is wrong in your body. Many different things can cause stom-achaches—being nervous about a big test at school, eating certain foods, eating too quickly, or eating too much. You can even get a stomachache when you're very hungry.

Did You Know...

After the common cold, stomachaches are the most common reason why people go to see health care providers. About 95 million Americans have some kind of digestive problem.

◀ **Sometimes stomachaches can feel so uncomfortable that you have to lie down.**

Often a stomachache is caused by a problem in your **digestive system**. This system breaks food down into tiny bits your body can use. Normally, you don't even notice that this is happening. Your stomach and other digestive organs work automatically without your having to think about them. You are aware of them only when something goes wrong, such as when you get a stomachache.

Most stomachaches are not serious. Sometimes an upset stomach goes away by itself in just a few hours or sooner. But some people have stomachaches so often that they feel like they are hurting all the time. When stomach problems won't go away, a health care provider can help to find out what is wrong and determine what can be done to help.

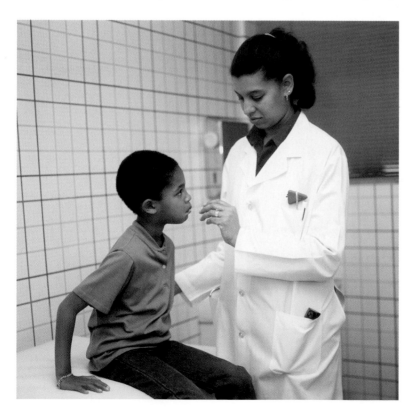

A health care provider may examine you to find the source of your stomach problems.

How Digestion Works

Do you know where your stomach is? Most people point to the belly button when asked that question. Actually, though, the stomach is higher, just below the ribs. Most of it is on the left side of the body. Underneath the stomach are the small and large intestines. The **intestines** arc long, coiled tubes that are packed inside your belly. You are pointing to your intestines when you are pointing to your belly button. And when you have a stomachache, the pain that you feel is probably coming from your intestines.

Your stomach is located just below your ribs, and your small and large intestines are below it.

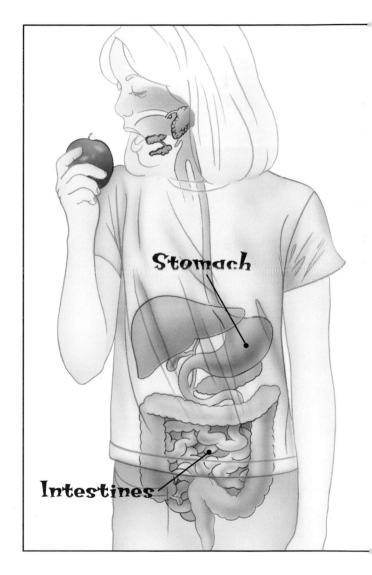

Stomach

Intestines

Stomachaches often occur when something has gone wrong during the digestion process. So before you can understand why you get stomachaches, you need to understand how digestion works.

Food provides your body with the energy it needs to keep you alive and moving. But even the tiniest crumb is too big to fit inside your body's cells. Your digestive system breaks down the food and turns it into a form the body can use.

When you eat a slice of pizza, your digestive system gets to work even before you take the first bite. Just one look at the dripping cheese and your mouth starts to produce watery **saliva**. Once the food enters your mouth, saliva mixes with the food, making it soft and moist. At the same time, your teeth cut and grind

Just the sight or smell of a tasty meal can start your digestive system working.

8

the food into smaller pieces. These pieces are slowly broken down as the food travels through a long passageway inside you, called the **digestive tract**. The digestive tract begins at the mouth and ends at the **anus**, an opening through which waste products leave the body.

As the food moves through the digestive tract, it is mixed with special chemicals called **enzymes**. These enzymes start to break down some of the materials in the food. This process starts in the mouth, while you chew. When you swallow a glob of food, it passes down a tube called the **esophagus**. As the food enters the esophagus, muscles in its wall contract (narrow), pushing the food downward. The contractions continue until the food is pushed through the entire 10-inch (25-centimeter) length of the esophagus.

9

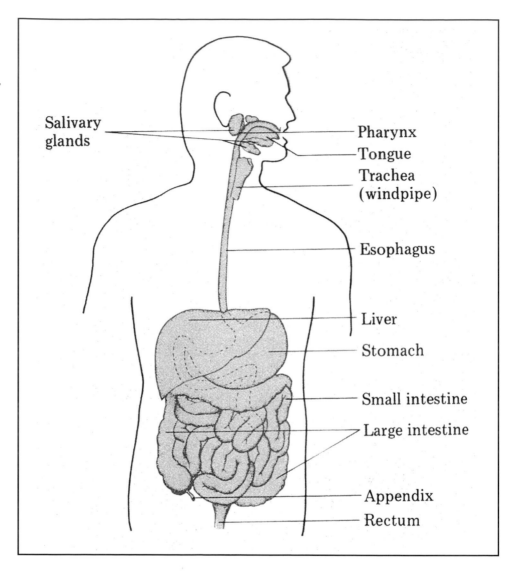

Salivary
glands

Pharynx

Tongue

Trachea
(windpipe)

Esophagus

Liver

Stomach

Small intestine

Large intestine

Appendix

Rectum

At the end of the esophagus is a strong ring of muscle called the **cardiac sphincter**. The cardiac part of the name comes from the fact that it is near the heart. When the sphincter relaxes, the opening widens and food squirts into the stomach. The stomach expands as it fills up with food, just like a balloon expands when you fill it with air. Much of the stomach is made up of powerful muscles. The stomach muscles contract, mixing and churning the stomach's contents. Meanwhile, the stomach lining releases acid and more enzymes into the food, turning it into a soupy liquid. This partly digested food is squirted, a little at a time, into a long, thin, coiled tube called the small intestine.

Nearby organs, the **pancreas** and *liver*, release more digestive enzymes into the small intestine that continue breaking down the food. Most digestion occurs in the small intestine, where enzymes help to split food materials into small chemicals. These food chemicals pass through the walls of the small intestine into the bloodstream. As blood flows through your body, these food chemicals are delivered to the cells.

Activity 1:
See Digestion at Work

Laundry detergents usually contain enzymes that get rid of stains by breaking down proteins and fats, in much the same way that enzymes in the intestines digest proteins and fat in the food you eat. You can watch digestion in action with this activity. Mix a tablespoon of detergent into a glass of warm water. Then cut a hard-boiled egg into slices and put them into the mixture. (You should have an adult help you boil your egg.) Let it stand for a few days, checking the size and appearance of the egg slices every day. Notice the effect the enzymes have on the egg slices. Egg white is almost pure protein, and the yolk is high in fat.

Food that cannot be digested continues on into a short, wide, looping tube called the large intestine. Extra liquid and vitamins are removed from the undigested food material by the large intestine and sent into the bloodstream. What's left over is waste, which eventually leaves your body as **feces**.

The Creatures Inside Your Small Intestine

You have probably heard about bacteria, the tiny germs that make people sick. But there are some kinds of bacteria that live in your intestines and are not harmful at all. In fact, they help you. Some of them help to destroy "bad" bacteria and other tiny creatures that could be harmful to you. Others make important vitamins, such as different kinds of B vitamins and vitamin K, which keep you healthy and strong. They live so well feeding off the undigested food in the large intestine that they multiply to enormous numbers. In fact, bacteria make up 20 to 50 percent of the feces that pass out of your body.

Is It Something You Ate?

"Excuse me," you say automatically when you let out a loud burp. People often see burping as a sign of bad manners, but everybody does it. Burping usually occurs during or after eating a meal because you swallow some air when you eat or drink.

Inside your stomach, the air forms gas bubbles that build up and press outward on the stomach walls. Finally, the cardiac sphincter—the muscle at the end

Carbonated beverages can form gas bubbles in your stomach.

of the esophagus—pops open, and a big gas bubble explodes up through the esophagus and out your mouth. Colas and other carbonated soft drinks can make you burp too. These drinks contain a gas that comes bubbling out when you drink it.

Gases may also be produced when foods are digested. Most of the gas in your intestines is produced by bacteria as they feed on food materials. Some foods are known for being gas producers, such as beans, broccoli, cabbage, and onions. The gas bubbles continue to move through the body until eventually they pass out of the body through the anus. When you pass gas, it is often rather smelly because some of the gases produced by the bacteria in the intestines have strong odors.

Gas may be embarrassing at times, but it's normal. Sometimes, however, gas can cause you problems, especially when gas bubbles get trapped inside the stomach or intestines. As the gas bubbles build up, they create pressure against the stomach or intestinal wall. This pressure can be very uncomfortable, and even painful.

Did You Know...

If you think you have too much gas, consider this: It is normal to pass gas fourteen to twenty-three times a day.

Many people get **indigestion** from time to time. Indigestion is a feeling of discomfort or pain in the abdomen (belly). Sometimes it may even make people feel like vomiting. Indigestion usually occurs after you eat or drink too much, which puts pressure on the stomach muscles. You can also get indigestion from eating so fast that you swallow a lot of air, making your stomach feel full and bloated. Sometimes you may feel better after burping or passing gas.

Spicy foods, such as curry or chili, can damage the stomach lining and make your stomach ache. Alcohol and some medicines, such as aspirin, can also irritate your

Indigestion can cause painful stomachaches.

stomach. So can germs, such as bacteria and viruses, which can make the cells in the stomach lining swollen and painful.

Heartburn often occurs along with indigestion. It actually has nothing to do with the heart. When the cardiac sphincter is not closed tightly enough, stomach acid may splash up into the esophagus, causing a burning feeling in the middle of the chest.

The Acid in Your Stomach

The acid produced in your stomach is so powerful that it could burn a hole in a carpet or melt away the iron in a nail. So why doesn't it damage your stomach? The delicate cells in your stomach lining are protected by a coating of thick, gooey mucus. The lining of your esophagus does not have this protective coating. That's why heartburn hurts so much.

Sometimes the stress from schoolwork or other problems can cause stomach pains.

Not all stomachaches are caused by something you ate. Actually, stress is one of the most common causes of stomachaches in kids. Stress is a normal part of life. But too much stress can cause problems. Worrying about things like tests, schoolwork, threats from a bully, trouble at home, or problems with friends can have a bad effect on your digestive tract and other parts of your body. When you worry too much, your stomach muscles start to tighten up, causing pain. Stress can also make your stomach produce too much acid, which may lead to stomach problems.

Have you ever heard people say, "Don't worry so much. You're going to give yourself an ulcer"? An **ulcer** is a sore in the lining of the stomach or the **duodenum** (the first part of the small intestine). Many people think that ulcers are things that only adults with high-stress jobs get. The truth is, though, that anyone can get ulcers—even kids.

Medical experts used to think that ulcers were caused by too much stress. But now they know that most adults get ulcers from a bacterium called *Helicobacter pylori (H. pylori)*. Researchers have found that lots of people carry the H. pylori bacterium, but most of them do not develop ulcers. Medical experts do not understand why this happens. This bacterium is often the cause of ulcers in adults, but not in most cases of ulcers in children. Many ulcer cases in children do not have a known cause. Doctors believe that some ulcers may be caused by overusing pain relievers, such as aspirin or ibuprofen.

Some people may develop ulcers because they take aspirin too frequently.

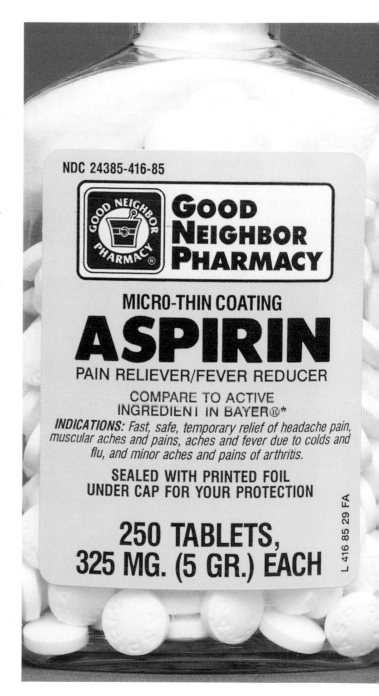

An ulcer develops when the body can't make enough mucus to protect the sensitive lining of the stomach and duodenum from stomach acid. While stress may not cause ulcers to develop, the extra acid produced when people feel stress can make ulcers worse. The chemicals in aspirin and some other pain relievers can also damage the stomach lining. *H. pylori* bacteria burrow through the mucus that coats the lining and settle down to multiply. They irritate the delicate cells on their own, and the holes

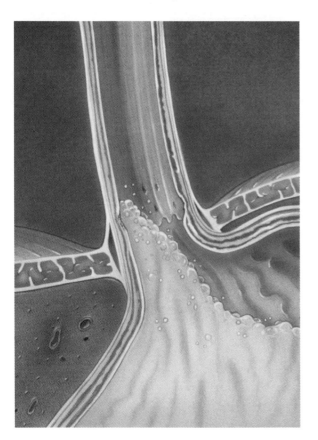

Ulcers can form when acid reaches the sensitive lining of the stomach and duodenum.

they made in the mucus allow acid to get in. Soon an ulcer develops. Ulcers usually cause a burning pain in the upper abdomen, between the chest and the belly button.

Pain that begins around the belly button and then moves down to the lower right part of the abdomen may be caused by **appendicitis**. If you also have a fever, a loss of appetite, and vomiting, you should see a health care provider right away.

Your body gets rid of wastes on a regular basis. You probably have a **bowel movement** once a day. A bowel movement is important because it gets rid of the feces or stool that is produced in your large intestine. But sometimes things don't work the way they are supposed to, and you might develop **diarrhea** or **constipation**.

Diarrhea occurs when the large intestine moves food wastes along too quickly. The stool is watery, and you need to go to the bathroom frequently. When you have diarrhea, your body loses a lot of water. Losing too much water can be very danger- ous, especially if it continues for a long time. So, if

It is impor- tant to drink lots of fluids if you have diarrhea so that you do not become dehydrated.

you have diarrhea, make sure to drink lots of liquids. Diarrhea may be caused by medications, unclean food or drink, bacteria, viruses, or stress.

Constipation is a condition in which food wastes stay in the large intestine for too long. The stool becomes dry, and it is too painful to pass out of the body. When you ignore your body's signals for a bowel movement, water is removed from the feces. Water keeps the feces soft and helps them to pass out of the body comfortably. Hard feces make it difficult to have regular bowel movements. After a while, you may start having cramps, bloating, and pain in the abdomen.

Diarrhea and constipation can cause stomach pains.

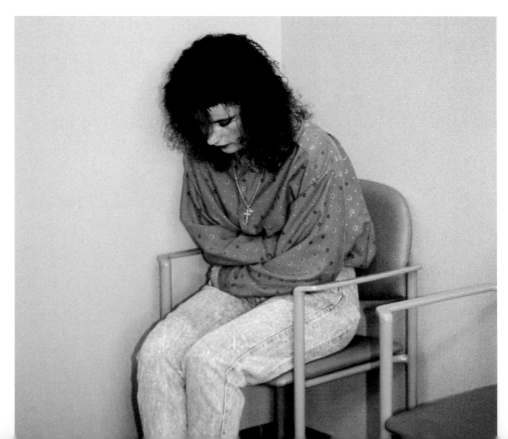

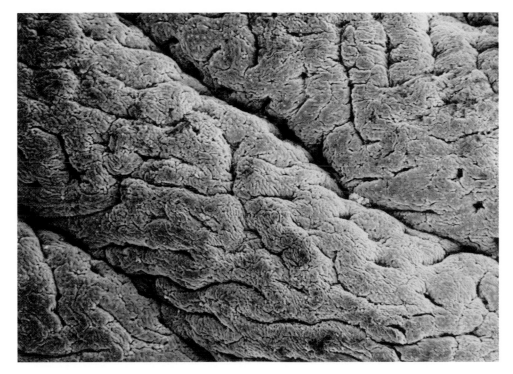

Sometimes diarrhea and constipation may be signs of other conditions. For example, **irritable bowel syndrome** (IBS) is a condition in which the **colon**, a major part of the large intestine, isn't working properly. Medical experts don't know exactly what causes IBS. What they do know is that people with IBS have colons that are very sensitive and react to things that wouldn't bother most people. For example, caffeine, chocolate, and milk products may bring on symptoms such as cramps, stomach pain, gassiness, bloating, and problems with bowel movements.

Foods Your Body Can't Handle

Many people get stomach problems when they eat certain foods because they have an **allergy** to them. An allergy causes your body to overreact to a substance that does not normally bother most people. If someone has an allergy to strawberries, for example, eating a couple of them may give this person a bad stomachache.

There are also people who can't drink milk or other dairy products. Their bodies have a problem digesting these foods properly. These people have a condition called **lactose intolerance**. Milk contains lactose, which is a milk sugar. Lactose-intolerant people don't have an enzyme called lactase, which is needed to digest milk products. So when they drink milk or eat cheese or ice cream, they may get a stomachache, gas, or diarrhea.

Eating ice cream may cause stomachaches for people who are lactose intolerant.

Seeking Help

Although millions of people get stomachaches, health care providers don't hear about most of them. Most people get stomachaches only once in a while, and they usually don't last very long. But if you get stomachaches often, or if they make it hard for you to live normally, then you should see a health care provider.

Stomachaches can be caused by any number of things. Your health care provider will need to collect information to zero in on a possible cause. When did the stomachaches start? When do they occur? After a meal? How often do they occur? Where exactly is the pain? In the chest? Behind the belly button? How would you describe the pain? Dull or sharp? Mild or severe? Are there any other symptoms? The medical expert may also ask if other members of

Frequent stomachaches may be a sign of serious problems and should be checked by a health care provider.

your family have had stomach problems. Certain kinds of digestive problems run in families.

Getting a physical exam that pays special attention to the organs of the digestive system can also help to rule out possible health problems. There are a number of ways to get a close-up look at the digestive tract to see what's going on. One way is to run a **GI series**. (GI stands for "gastrointestinal.") This is a series of X rays that shows the upper and lower digestive tract. The digestive organs are made of soft tissues and normally would not show up on an X ray. To make these tissues show up clearly, you swallow a flavored "milkshake" containing the chemical barium sulfate, which helps to outline the esophagus, stomach, and duodenum as the drink moves down through each digestive organ.

A GI series will help doctors examine the organs of your digestive system.

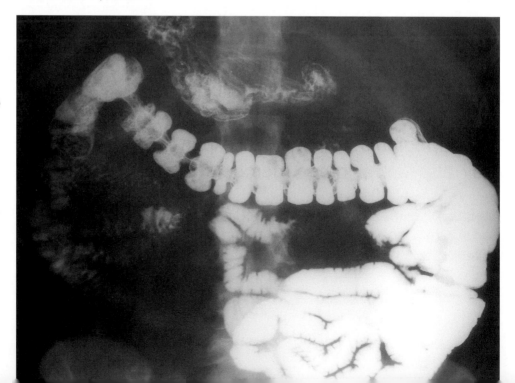

There are also instruments that allow a health care provider to actually look into the digestive tract and snip off bits of tissue for testing. An **endoscope** is a long, flexible tube with a tiny camera on the end. This instrument is inserted through the mouth and threaded down your throat and into your stomach and duodenum. It can be used to check the lining of the esophagus, stomach, and duodenum for possible ulcers or swelling. The endoscope may also be used to take tissue samples to check for the *H. pylori* bacterium. A special probe is often used to measure the amount of acid being produced in the stomach. This isn't as scary as it sounds—you probably won't be awake during the procedure, and you won't feel anything.

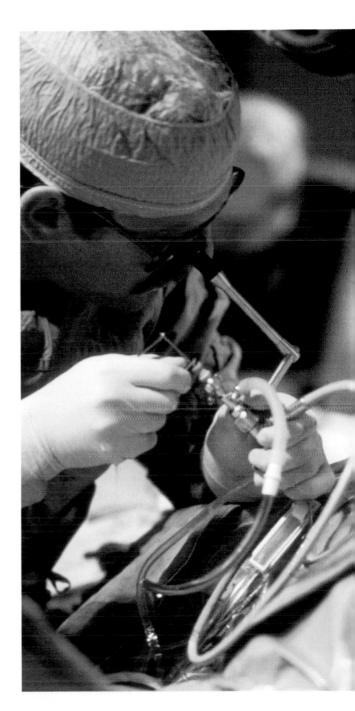

This doctor is using an endoscope to check his patient for ulcers.

Swallowing a Camera

Wouldn't it be great if medical experts could watch a movie of a trip through the whole digestive tract and spot anything wrong in your stomach and intestines? An endoscope does part of the job, but it only reaches down to the duodenum.

Recently, researchers have developed a video

This quarter-sized camera can travel through the digestive system and photograph the entire journey.

camera so small that it can fit into a capsule the size of a vitamin pill. The patient swallows the capsule, and it travels down the esophagus to the stomach, through the coiling small intestine, around the loops of the large intestine, and finally out through the anus. As it goes, the camera takes hundreds of full-color pictures each minute and transmits them to a receiver worn on the patient's belt. A computer puts these pictures together into a video tour of the small intestine. The Food and Drug Administration approved the new device in 2001, after tests showed that it can find ulcers and other gastrointestinal problems even better than can an endoscope.

If the health care provider suspects that you have an ulcer, blood tests and breath tests may also be used to detect *H. pylori*.

It is very important to identify exactly what is causing your stomachaches because different causes require different treatments. For example, an ulcer that is caused by *H. pylori* must be treated differently than one that is caused by overuse of aspirin. It is also best to get a diagnosis early on, so that the problem does not become more difficult to treat.

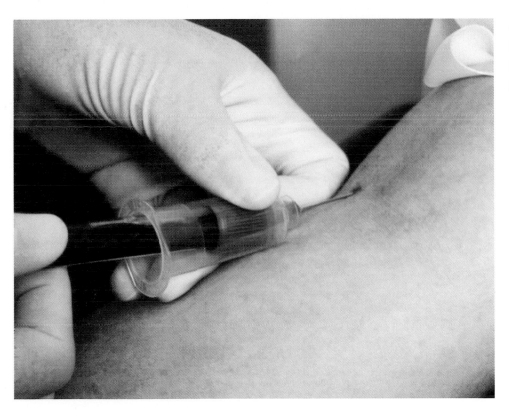

A blood test may be necessary to check for H. pylori.

Treating Stomachaches

Most stomachaches are not serious and can be treated at home. Some people use ginger, an herb that has healing properties. Drinking flat ginger ale is a well-known treatment for soothing an upset stomach. (Bubbly ginger ale would just add gas to an already aching stomach.) Eating a few ginger snaps or drinking herbal tea sprinkled with powdered ginger can also help to settle your stomach. You also may get some

Some types of tea may sooth an upset stomach.

relief from drinking chamomile or peppermint tea. Putting a hot water bottle on your belly may also help make a stomachache feel better.

The Milk Myth

Medical experts used to think that drinking milk helped to calm an upset stomach. This is not true. In fact, researchers have found that milk actually *increases* stomach acid levels, especially in people with ulcers. Research also showed that the healing process was much slower in people who drank milk than those who stayed away from it. Ulcers often did not heal completely in the milk drinkers. Interestingly, the milk drinkers said they found that drinking milk eased the pain. This pain relief may have helped to keep the milk myth going.

It is not a good idea to drink milk if you have ulcers.

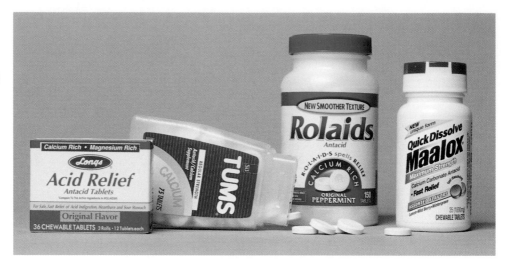

Many people take over-the-counter medications, such as **antacids**, to treat their heartburn or indigestion. Antacids contain chemicals that change stomach acid into a harmless form so that it doesn't hurt the sensitive stomach lining. There are also drugs that help stop diarrhea by making the intestines less "irritable" and slowing down the contractions that move food along. Constipation can be treated with drugs called **laxatives**, which make intestinal contractions stronger. Foods, powders, and pills that make the feces softer can also help relieve constipation. All of these remedies are usually fast and effective. Although a prescription is not needed for these products, you should talk to a health care provider before treating a stomach problem on your own.

Antacids Are Not Candy

Antacid tablets come in a variety of tasty flavors, so it may be easy to forget that you're taking medicine, not candy. Popping a couple of antacid tablets after a spicy meal is okay every once in a while, but taking too many of them for a long time can lead to serious health problems. Most antacids contain calcium, which is normally good for you, but if it's taken in large amounts for months or years, it may cause kidney stones, which can be very painful.

An ulcer is a serious condition. How it's treated will depend on what caused it. For example, ulcers that are caused by *H. pylori* are treated with **antibiotics**, which are medicines used to kill bacteria. Along with antibiotics, the doctor may also prescribe drugs to reduce the production of stomach acid. Antibiotics will not work for ulcers that are caused by the irritating effects of aspirin and other painkillers, but the condition will get better when the person stops taking these medicines. Drugs that reduce stomach acid can also help in the treatment process. It may take up to eight weeks for an ulcer to heal. The health care provider will probably want to use an endoscope several months after treatment to make sure the ulcer is healing properly.

There are no drugs that can treat irritable bowel syndrome, which affects millions of people. But the condition can be helped by eating a well-balanced diet that includes **fiber**. Fiber, a tough part of food that cannot be digested, soaks up water as it passes through the stomach and intestines. The undigested food matter swells up and fills your intestines. This gives the muscles in the intestinal walls a signal to start working and move things along. The water held by the fiber keeps the feces soft, so that it can move easily. Good sources of fiber are fruits, vegetables, and whole-grain breads and cereals. Fiber supplements, such as bran (the outer husks of wheat, oats, or other grains) and various powders and pills can also help ease irritable bowel syndrome.

Eating lots of fruits and vegetables is a good way to get fiber.

Fiber is a good remedy for constipation too. But remember: Always drink a lot of liquid when you take extra fiber. Otherwise it will just lump up into a hard mass and make you even more constipated. It is not a good idea to take laxatives such as milk of magnesia very often. These drugs usually work by irritating the digestive system so that it moves food matter along more quickly. But if you take laxatives too often, your intestines may get lazy and stop working regularly on their own. Overusing laxatives may also prevent your body from getting enough nourishment, because food is moved through your digestive tract and out of the body before it has been fully digested. Fiber does not cause these problems. It is a natural way to get your digestive system working regularly again.

Did You Know...

Scientists say that early humans ate a diet that contained a lot more fiber than the diet we eat today.

Take Care of Yourself

Almost everybody gets a stomachache now and then. But you can avoid a lot of stomach problems by learning good eating habits.

Have you ever been told to eat slowly? When you gobble down food, you swallow a lot of extra air, which may cause gas bubbles to build up inside your stomach or intestinal walls. Then you get gas pains. Make sure to eat slowly and chew your food thoroughly. Chewing helps to get the saliva flowing, which gets the digestion process going. Well-chewed food is soft and moist, which makes it easier to swallow and easier for the stomach juices to work on.

Eat slowly and chew your food well to prevent digestive problems.

Listen to your stomach. When you feel your stomach rumbling, it's trying to tell you, "I need food now!" Don't wait until you get hunger pains to eat. And when your stomach feels full, don't try to shovel in another couple of bites, even if you are eating your favorite food. Even a good meal isn't so good when you've had too much of it. You just end up with a stomachache.

Eating regularly is also very important. Health experts say that instead of eating three large meals each day, people should eat smaller meals spaced out throughout the day. This actually helps your digestive system to work better and keeps you regular. You should never skip meals. This can throw your body off schedule, and the digestion process may not work as smoothly.

Fatty foods take longer to digest, and they may irritate the intestines. So cut down on those cheeseburgers and french fries if you want to keep your digestive system trouble-free.

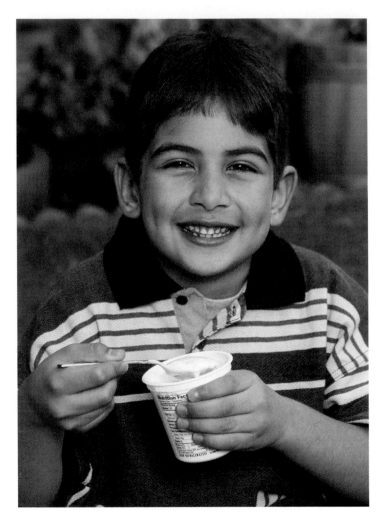

Foods that contain fiber, such as whole grains, vegetables, and fruits, can help you avoid stomachaches, even though you can't digest the fiber at all. You may have heard that high-fiber foods provide "bulk." That means that the fiber draws in water and gets larger. Doctors say that eating foods with a lot of fiber every day helps to keep your digestion regular. Plenty of fiber in your diet will help you to avoid constipation and diarrhea. The feces produced from a high-fiber diet are soft, but still solid—not runny—because the fiber soaks up any excess water.

Yogurt is another food that may help prevent digestive problems. This milk product contains bacteria that help protect you from some kinds of germs that can make you ill.

Activity 2: Keep a Food Diary

Keep a diary of all the foods you eat throughout the day for a week. Each day, write down the time that you eat and list the foods you eat. Write down if you notice any problems within an hour of that meal. Did you have stomach pains? Did you pass a lot of gas? Did you have diarrhea? If you didn't notice any obvious problem, write down "none." At the end of the week, take a look at your food diary. Did any foods give you stomach problems? Which foods gave you a lot of gas? You should probably stay away from any foods that gave you serious problems.

Everyone knows that exercise is a great way to get physically fit. But did you know that exercise also helps in digestion? Regular exercise helps to keep food moving along through your digestive tract. You don't have to run every day to get a good workout.

Playing sports and other exercises will keep the food moving through your digestive system.

Anything that gets you moving is exercise—playing sports, running around, or even walking the dog.

Exercise also helps your mind. When you exercise, your body makes chemicals called **endorphins**. Endorphins work in your brain to make you feel good. So after a stressful day, exercise can make you feel calm and happy.

Breathing exercises also calm you down when you are stressed out. When you breathe, you take in oxygen, which is used by your body cells to create energy. Breathing deeply brings more oxygen into the body and makes you feel calmer. Controlling stress also helps your digestive system work better.

A healthy digestive system is a part of a healthy body. Your body will give you clues to what makes it feel good or bad. Learning to understand these signals and paying attention to them will help to keep all of your body's systems running smoothly.

Glossary

allergy—a sensitivity to a certain substance that would not cause a reaction in most people

antacids—medicine containing chemicals that work to treat excess stomach acid

antibiotics—medicines used to kill bacteria

anus—the opening through which undigested food materials leave the body

appendicitis—pain and swelling in the appendix, a small, tubelike branch of the small intestine

bowel movement—getting rid of the body's wastes from the digestive tract by pushing feces out through the anus

cardiac sphincter—the ring of muscle surrounding the opening from the esophagus into the stomach

colon—the first part of the large intestine

constipation—the failure to have regular bowel movements

diarrhea—frequent soft or liquid bowel movements

digestive system—the group of organs that break food down into smaller parts that the body can use for energy or building materials

digestive tract—the tubelike passageway inside the body in which food is digested. It extends from the mouth to the anus and includes the esophagus, stomach, and intestines.

duodenum—the first part of the small intestine

endorphins—chemicals released in the body that send "happy messages" to the brain

endoscope—a long tube equipped with a camera that is used to see the inside of the digestive tract

enzyme—A chemical that helps break down foods in the body

esophagus—the tube leading from the mouth to the stomach

feces—body wastes (undigested food matter and bacteria) formed in the large intestine

fiber—the indigestible parts of plants eaten as foods

GI series—a series of X rays showing the organs of the digestive tract

heartburn—a burning feeling felt in the front of the chest caused by the splashing of stomach acid up into the esophagus

indigestion—a feeling of discomfort or pain in the abdomen

intestines—coiled, tubelike parts of the digestive tract in which food is digested and food materials are absorbed

irritable bowel sydrome (IBS)—a chronic (ongoing) condition of the colon

lactose intolerance—a condition in which the body is unable to digest lactose, a sugar found in milk and other dairy products

laxative—a drug that relieves constipation

liver—a large organ that produces a digestive juice, bile, and does a variety of other jobs

pancreas—an organ that produces digestive juices and makes hormones such as insulin (which helps to control the amount of glucose in the blood)

saliva—a watery fluid that contains digestive enzymes and is produced in the mouth

ulcer—a sore in the lining of the stomach or duodenum

Learning More

Books

Avraham, Regina. *The Digestive System*. Philadelphia, PA: Chelsea House Publishers, 2000.

Goldentyes, Debra. *Stress (Preteen Pressures)*. New York: Raintree/Steck Vaughn, 1998.

Janowitz, Henry D. *Indigestion*. New York: Oxford University Press, 1992.

Lipski, Elizabeth. *Digestive Wellness*. New Canaan, CT: Keats Publishing, Inc., 1996.

Monroe, Judy. *Ulcers, Heartburn, and Stress-Related Stomach Disorders*. New York: Rosen Publishing Group, Inc., 2000.

Stille, Darlene R. *The Digestive System*. New York: Children's Press, 1997.

Turiello, James. *Learning How We Digest (The 3-D Library of the Human Body)*. New York: Rozen Publishing Group, 2002.

Organizations and Online Sites

The American Dietetic Association
216 West Jackson Blvd., Ste. 800
Chicago, IL 60606-6995
(312) 899-0040

Are Your Bowels Moving?
http://kidshealth.org/kid/stay_healthy/body/bowel.html
Information for kids about constipation and diarrhea.

Ask NOAH About: Stomach and Intestinal Disorders
http://www.noah-health.org/english/illness/gastro/gastro.html
Links to dozens of articles about digestive system problems.

How Does Your Stomach Keep From Digesting Itself?
http://www.howstuffworks.com/question464.htm
Information about the stomach and ulcers from the "How Stuff Works" series by Marshall Brain.

The Real Deal on the Digestive System
http://kidshealth.org/kid/body/digest_noSW_p2.html
Information for kids on the parts of the digestive system, what they do, and how to keep them healthy.

Stomach Gurgles
http://yucky.kids.discovery.com/noflash/body/yuckystuff/gurgle/js.index.html
Listen to a stomach gurgle and read about why your stomach gurgles, then click on the links to find more fun stuff about the digestive system.

Index

About the Authors

Dr. Alvin Silverstein is a professor of biology at the College of Staten Island of the City University of New York. **Virginia B. Silverstein** is a translator of Russian scientific literature. The Silversteins first worked together on a research project at the University of Pennsylvania. Since then, they have produced 6 children and more than 180 published books for young people.

Laura Silverstein Nunn, a graduate of Kean College, has been helping with her parents' books since her high-school days. She is the coauthor of more than 50 books on diseases and health, science concepts, endangered species, and pets. Laura lives with her husband, Matt, and their young son, Cory, in a rural New Jersey town not far from her childhood home.